ARITHMETIC

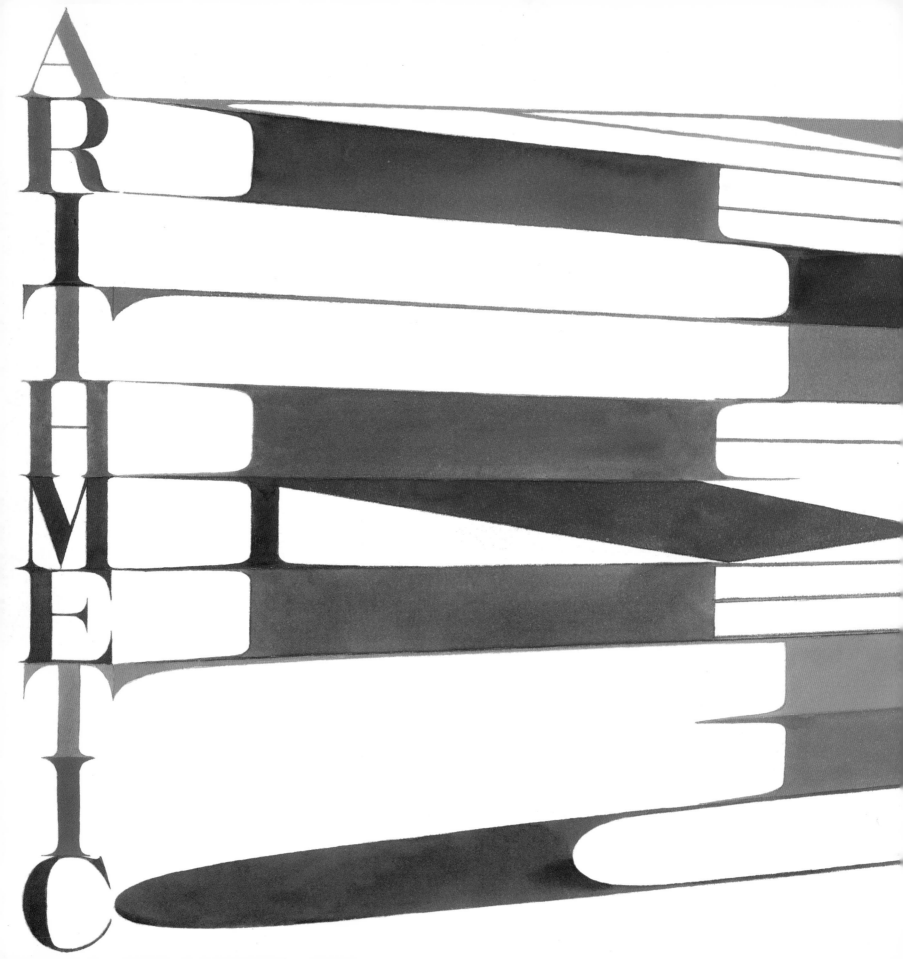

CARL SANDBURG

Illustrated as an anamorphic adventure by

TED RAND

Harcourt Brace Jovanovich, Publishers

San Diego   New York   London

Printed in Singapore

Arithmetic is where numbers fly like pigeons
in and out of your head.

Arithmetic tells you how many you lose or win
if you know how many you had
before you lost or won.

Arithmetic is seven eleven
all good children go to heaven—

or five six bundle of sticks.

Arithmetic is numbers you squeeze from your head to your hand to your pencil to your paper till you get the answer.

Arithmetic is where the answer is right and everything is nice and you can look out of the window and see the blue sky—

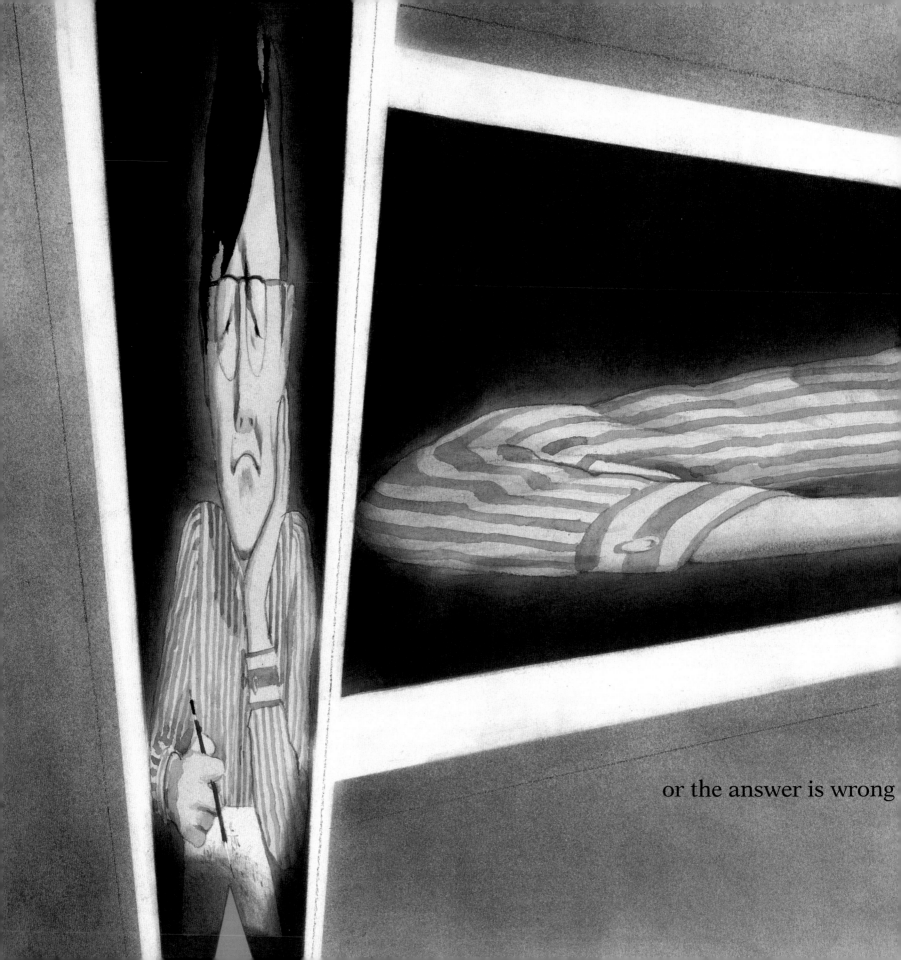

or the answer is wrong

and you have to start all over and try again and see how it comes out this time.

If you take a number and double it and double it again $1\ 2\ 4\ 8\ 16\ 32\ 64$

128 256 512 1024

2048 40

and then double it a few more times, the number

6810921638

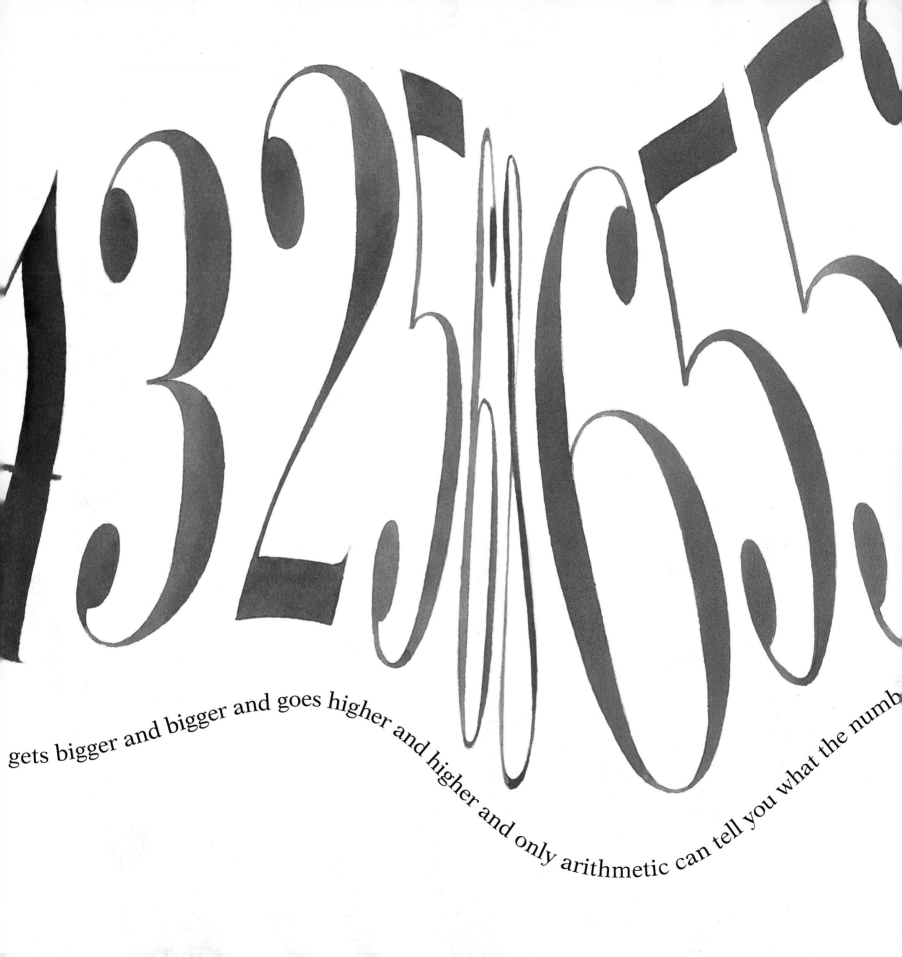

gets bigger and bigger and goes higher and higher and only arithmetic can tell you what the numb

262144524288104

s when you decide to quit doubling.

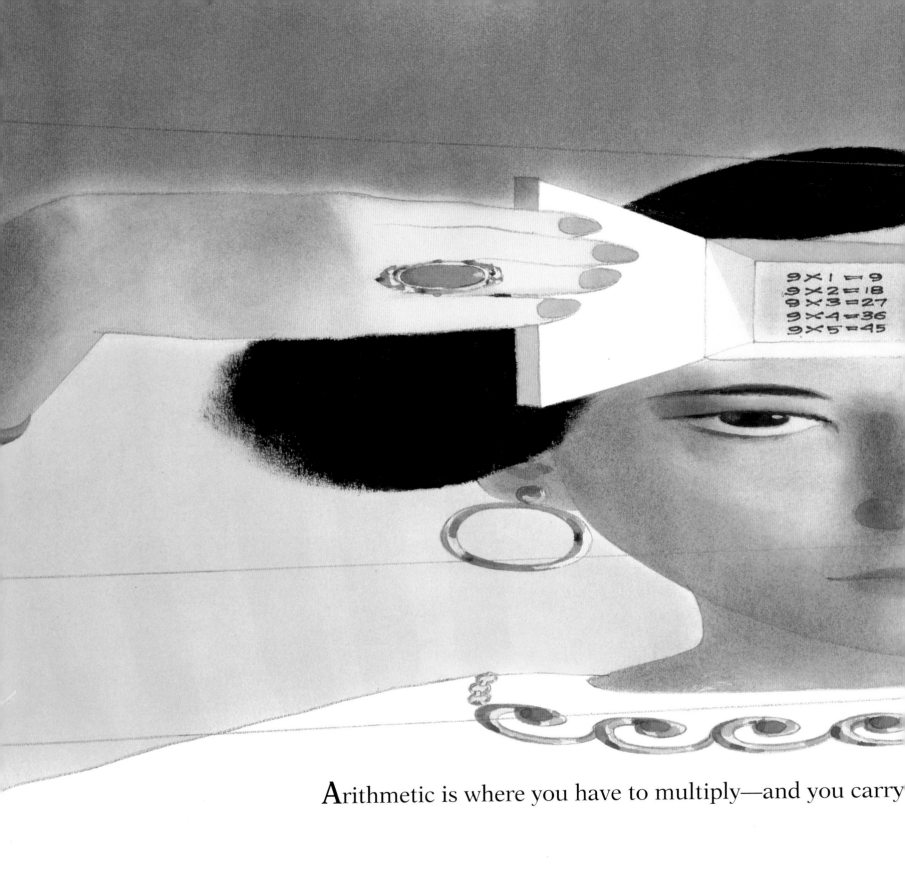

9 X 1 = 9
9 X 2 = 18
9 X 3 = 27
9 X 4 = 36
9 X 5 = 45

Arithmetic is where you have to multiply—and you carry

the multiplication table in your head and hope you won't lose it.

If you have two animal crackers, one good and one bad, and you eat one and a striped zebra with streaks all over him eats the other, how many animal crackers will you have if somebody offers you five six seven

and you say NO NO NO and you say NAY NAY NAY

and you say NIX NIX NIX?

If you ask your mother for one fried egg for breakfast and she gives you two fried

Place cylinder here

eggs and you eat both of them, who is better at arithmetic, you or your mother?

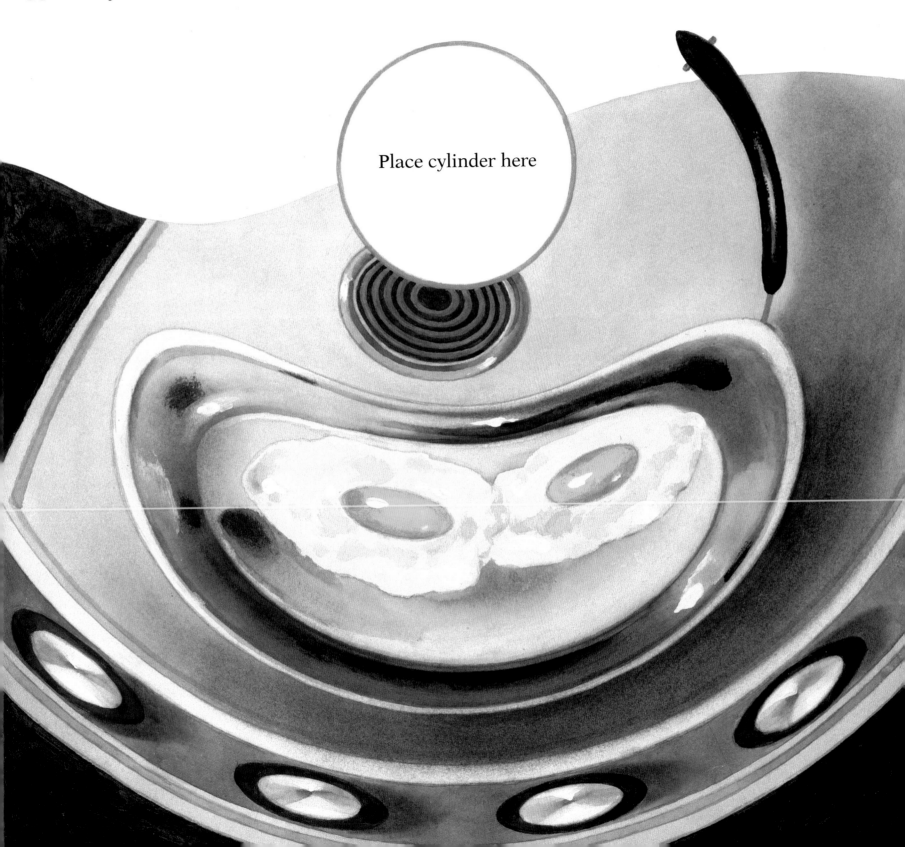

Place cylinder here

Anamorphic: *Formed anew. An anamorphic drawing shows a distortion of the optical image. Some anamorphic drawings are made so that the distorted image can be restored to normal by viewing from a particular angle, or by viewing the image's reflection in a cylinder or cone.*

Most people are "lazy lookers." We look for what we expect to see and our mind's eye helps us by automatically correcting the image to what it "ought" to be. And so we miss many of the wonders and fascinating designs all around us. Look at streetlights reflected in puddles. Watch your shadow dance, look at objects through water, see your face mirrored in the back of a spoon. Often the distorted image—like your reflection in a funhouse mirror—is exciting!

Anamorphic techniques of drawing gained attention in Europe and China in the fifteenth century, soon after artists had rediscovered perspective. The famous Dutch artist Hans Holbein incorporated anamorphic images into some of his paintings. People have enjoyed experimenting with anamorphics ever since that time.

The pictures in *Arithmetic* may surprise you and help you see things as you have never seen them before. There are two primary ways to view the pictures in this book:

Hold the book open, close one eye, and look at the image with your eye near the red arrow.

Take the Mylar sheet out of its pocket and wrap it around a soda can. Place the Mylar cylinder on the circle that reads "Place cylinder here" and look at the reflected image.

Some pages show combinations of two or more different distortions, and others show distortions on the surface of the paper, as though the page had bubbled up or was rippled. Still others merely show you a familiar shape in a new form.

Any way you look at it, there are many challenges to be found in the pages of *Arithmetic*!

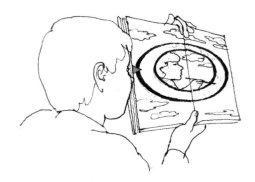

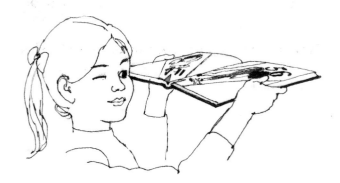

You can make your own anamorphic drawings by following these diagrams:

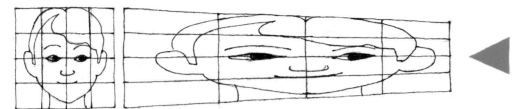

Make a grid over your drawing. Then draw a stretched grid next to the first one and stretch out your original drawing by copying the portion of the drawing from each square onto the same section of the new grid. The grid can be stretched in any direction.

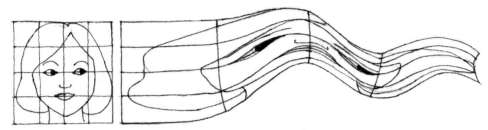

Draw a grid over a picture as you did above. Then draw a rippled grid next to the first one and transfer your original drawing, as above, onto the new grid. The rippled grid can be distorted any way you like. Use your imagination.

Draw a circle on your paper, wrap the Mylar sheet around a soda can, and place the Mylar cylinder on the circle. Then draw a picture, looking at the reflection of your work and not at the paper on which you are drawing. When you look at your finished picture without the cylinder, it will appear distorted.

To Gloria, for her love and encouragement

—T. R.

Library of Congress Cataloging-in-Publication Data
Sandburg, Carl, 1878–1967.
Arithmetic/by Carl Sandburg; illustrated as an anamorphic
adventure by Ted Rand.
p.   cm.
Summary: An illustrated poem about numbers and their
characteristics.
ISBN 0-15-203865-5
1. Arithmetic — Juvenile poetry. 2. Children's poetry, American.
[1. Arithmetic — Poetry. 2. American poetry.] I. Rand, Ted, ill.
II. Title.
PS3537.A618A88   1993
811'.52 — dc20   92-5291

First edition   A B C D E

The illustrations in this book were done in transparent watercolor,
liquid dye, ground chalk, and Prismacolor pencil
on 100% rag cold-press board.
The display type was set in Stone Serif by HBJ
Photocomposition Center, San Diego, California.
The text type was set in New Aster by Thompson Type,
San Diego, California.
Color separations by Bright Arts, Ltd., Singapore
Printed and bound by Tien Wah Press, Singapore
Production supervision by Warren Wallerstein and David Hough
Designed by Lydia D'moch